Philip Tusa, Architect
Projects

by Philip M. Tusa

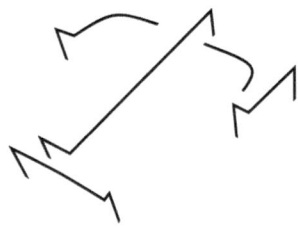

Philip Tusa
A R C H I T E C T

First published in the United
States of America in 2016
by Philip Tusa, Architect
   77 Old Post Road North
   Croton-on-Hudson, NY 10520
   www.philiptusa.com

ISBN 13: 978-0-578-69186-2

Table of Contents

Preface   4

Introduction   5

Commercial Projects   6

Dimitri Couture Showroom   8
Fruity's Restaurant   9
Playground Nightclub   10
The Left Bank Restaurant   11
Coney Island USA Freak Bar   12

Residential Projects   14

Clinton Avenue Apartment   16
Waterside Plaza Apartment   17
Roosevelt Island Apartment   18
Ottavi Firehouse Residence   19
Croton Cottage Residence   20

Corporate Projects   22

East 53rd Street Design Studio   24
Arnold Palmer Enterprises Offices   25
Gallucci Photo Studio   26
Saatchi & Saatchi Offices   27
5th Avenue Penthouse Studio   28

Landmark Projects   30

Grand Central Racquetball Club   32
NY Public Library-ITG Data Center   33
Queens Museum of Art   34
World Trade Center Memorial   35
Coney Island Parachute Pavilion   36

International Projects   38
Credits, Chronology   44

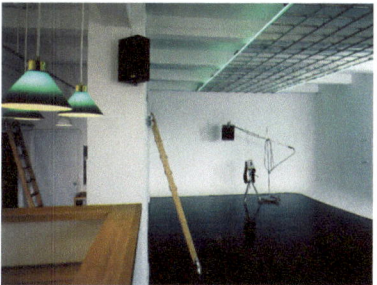

Preface

The purpose of this book is twofold. First, it is a retrospective survey of important projects and second, it serves as one part of a future trilogy of volumes that cover complementary aspects of practice. This "Projects" (Vol. 1) touches on topics in the forthcoming books "Renovating My New York" (Vol. 2) and "Travels To Cities & Buildings" (Vol. 3).

The survey covers projects created primarily for professional contract, but also includes selected projects for competition entries, academic credit and self-initiated endeavors. Besides these classifications, the projects are framed by time (the era of the 1960's to the present) and geography (mostly New York City & vicinity).

Organized by type, projects are grouped in four categories: Commercial (restaurants, bars, showrooms); Residential (houses, apartments); Corporate (offices, studios); Landmark (adapted for various uses).

Also, an International section with several European projects that anticipates the "Travel" (Vol. 3) subject matter.

Illustrations on this page show a selection of academic projects created from 1964 to 1973:

Clockwise from top left:
  1. Rockefeller Center drawing, 1964;
  2. Brownstone Garden model, 1967;
  3. Dining Room collage, 1969;
  4. Greenwich Ave. Cafe drawing, 1970;
  5. 16' Square House drawing; 1973;
  6. Clinton Hill Brownstone Apartment construction drawings, 1971, (see pages 14 & 16);
  7. Cobble Hill Brownstone model, 1970.

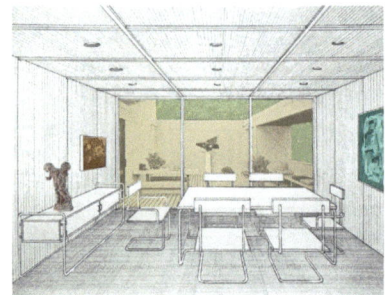

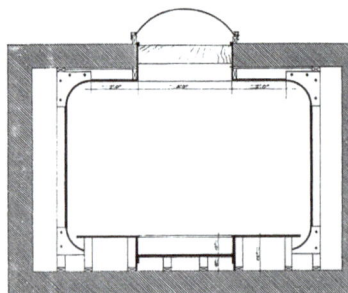

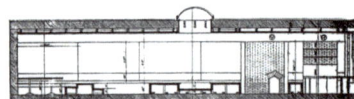

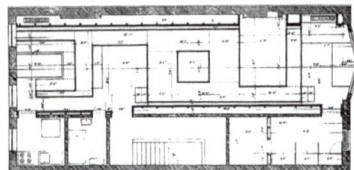

Introduction

The projects presented here are chosen to show the scope of the works accomplished over the years. They were created with the idea of applying an early ability to draw and build things and constantly develop those abilities through education and experience. The interweaving of architecture, interior design and renovation forms the theme of this collection and echoes each phase of education and practice.

Starting in Dyker Heights JHS art class (p.4, ill.1), on through the HS of Art & Design architecture program (p.4, ill.2), and then Pratt Institute interior design program (p.4, ill.3-7), the phases evolved from early academic to a first built project for credit (see pp.4-ill.6, 14 &16).

After 15 years of interior design practice and reaching a level of renovation requiring an architect, the next phase started by attending the Pratt School of Architecture for a first professional degree (1991), NYS license (1994) and a Master of Architecture (1998) with a Thesis entitled "Croton Neo-Arcadia".

Illustrations on this page show a selection of academic projects created from 1988 to 1998:

Clockwise from top left:
1. Speyer Synagogue Museum model, 1988, (see page 41);
2. DeMorgan's Law House drawing, 1989;
3. Broad Channel Civic Buildings model, 1989; 4. Park Slope Multi-use Complex model, 1990; 5. Geotarium Observatory model, 1990; 6. Croton Neo-Arcadia model, 1998; 7. Terracotta Artifact Museum collage, 1990; 8. Wood Detail House drawings, 1989.

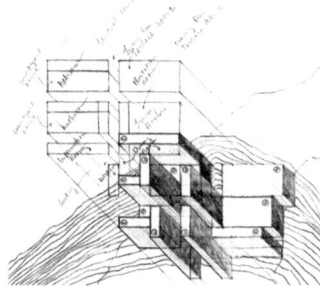

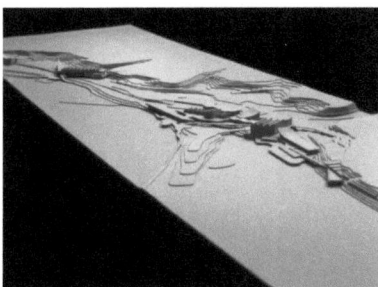

5

Commercial Projects

The term "commercial" is used here to connote a particular kind of business use that has public access, such as sidewalk exposure and oriented toward a transparent view, both outside in and inside out. Also considered public are business types such as showrooms and clubs that may be on a level other than the sidewalk but provides obvious public access.

Restaurants, clubs and bars are especially representative of this type and are featured prominently in this collection. Some of the characteristics that animate this type include the use of bold color, unique materials, and inventive detailing. The challenge is to orchestrate these elements into a cohesive distinctive theme.

Considering the specific contexts of these five projects, the most important is they're in prominent New York City commercial districts. The Dimitri Showroom (see p.8) is located on East 57th Street, a high-fashion avenue, just one block east of Tiffany's. It occupies the 5th floor in a strip of 19th century row houses (ill. top right). The floor plan delineates the main space with windows overlooking 57th Street (ill. top left).

Fruity's Restaurant, Juice Bar and Store (see p.9) is on East 53rd Street, two blocks from the fashionable Sutton Place. The neighborhood known as Turtle Bay is east of midtown and is a bustling area for a trendy health food restaurant. A large glass front entry welcomes all who stroll by (ill. middle right). The small late-19th-century loft building provides a layout with the store and juice bar upfront near the entry (ill. middle left).

Playground Nightclub (see p.10) is on the 2nd floor (ill. bottom left) of a building on West 22nd Street (ill. bottom right) 2 blocks west of the Flatiron Building.

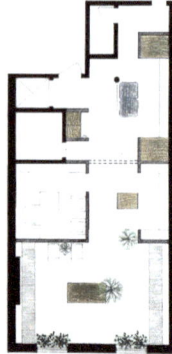

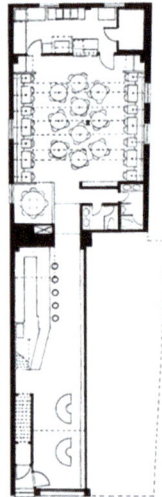

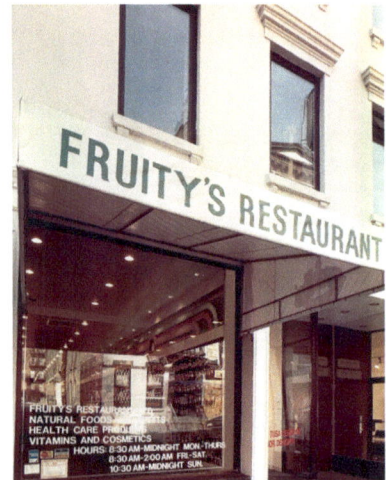

Commercial Projects continued

The Flatiron District is named after the Flatiron Building and was the tallest building in Manhattan at the time of completion in 1902. This neighborhood includes the Ladies Mile Historic District named after the many stores of that time clustered in the area.

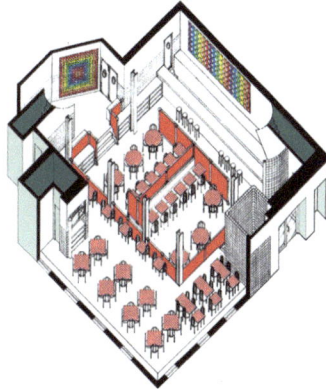

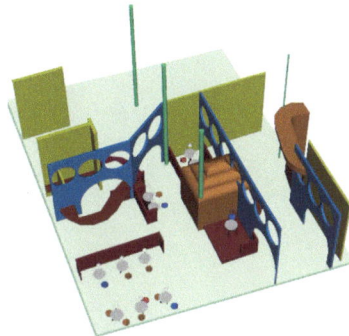

The Left Bank Restaurant (see p. 11) occupies the 1st floor of a 3-story brick building situated on the corner of 2nd Avenue at 64th Street (ill. top left). This area was known for a number of so-called singles bars, most famously T.G.I. Friday's and Maxwell's Plum. The layout (ill. top right) is organized by three zones: entry/bar, lower dining and upper dining. The upper part is four steps up and overlooks the sidewalk through french doors which swing inside 180 degrees.

Coney Island, the world-renowned playground of the masses is the quintessential place of commerce. Amusements and curiosties along with food and drink form the backdrop of this raucous and outlandish atmosphere. Coney Island USA is the arts organization that seeks to revive the iconic Coney with such events as the Mermaid Parade and Sideshows by the Seashore. The headquarters for CIUSA is the landmark Child's Building on Surf Avenue at West 12th Street (ill. bottom left). The Freak Bar & Museum Gift Shop (see p.12) serves as the public face of the organization and is front and center along the sidewalk that parallels the arched windows (ill. bottom right).

Taken together, these five projects represent a point of view that combines both renovation and urbanism. These two go hand in hand when the urban region is New York City and its thousands of buildings are in need of renovation or adaptive reuse. Up close, the excitement and stimulation of the New York City sidewalk enables the window shopper to peek through and see the inside and notice the buiding interior. Alternately, there are times when a diner is sitting by a window and watches the world go by.

Dimitri Couture Showroom

Coty Award winner Piero Dimitri needed more space as
he expanded his business as a master tailor to include
fashion design. The full-floor space, redesigned with
colleague Joseph Cerami, encompasses a showroom and
workspace. The front half is organized into a series
of areas accommodating the various clothing offerings,
divided by a progression of short white partitions set
against darker walls, ceiling, and floor. Strategically
placed mirrors give a feeling of space in tight areas.

Fruity's Restaurant & Store

The owner of this organic restaurant wished to avoid the somber, earth-tone decor long associated with typical health food restaurants. Thus, the emphasis is on bright, modern materials such as Pirelli studded rubber flooring and Plexiglas dividers. To bring sunlight into the rear dining room, newly discovered metal casement windows overlooking the gardens were restored. The front features an inviting entry with a juice bar and store that sells a variety of health food products and supplies.

Playground Nightclub

Playground is created on the second floor of a loft
building on West 22nd Street, near the former home of
the Ehrich Brother's Dry Goods Store when this
neighborhood was last fashionable as "Ladies Mile".
The crumbling loft space is neither gutted nor cleaned
up; instead, it is used as a gray backdrop for new blue
Plexiglas partitions that delineate intimate lounge and
table seating areas apart from the main dance floor.
As an echo, the bar area is lit by blue neon light tubes.

The Left Bank Restaurant

Fred Buchbinder, a restaurateur who previously owned The Right Bank Restaurant on Madison Avenue joined partner Kurt Kluger to open a companion restaurant, The Left Bank. The project transforms the dark, wood-paneled room to a bright, open atmosphere, oriented to the busy neighborhood through large windows. The elaborate bar from the original Metropolitan Opera House is reused here. Tables on two levels are divided by railings of red canvas panels laced to red pipes.

Coney Island USA New Freak Bar & Museum Gift Shop

CIUSA was awarded a city grant to purchase the Child's Building. The existing Freak Bar is expanded into the corner space and a New Museum Gift Shop is relocated from the 2nd floor to form a New Museum Entrance Lobby on the sidewalk level. Together, the new spaces form an interconnected whole that functions as CIUSA's "Front Door on Coney's Surf Avenue".

Freak Bar continued

Architecturally, this transformation is achieved by "perforating" the existing partitions with large-scale oculus and archway openings. Hidden underneath old plywood signs are arches of the landmark facade that are now revealed and incorporated. Decoratively, the "Coney-esque" style is employed. Historically, CIUSA seeks to evoke a nostalgic atmosphere that recalls a fun Coney to people worldwide. "Coney-esque" is colorful, bold, graphically abrasive, and spectacular day and night.

Residential Projects

Home is typically associated with the single-family house situated on a plot of land in a residential zone. But as cities developed and population density increased, the need to devise different kinds of housing to accommodate the change emerged. The five residences in this chapter are examples of this spectrum.

The classic row house is a type of urban housing prevalent in many neighborhoods of New York City. The Clinton Avenue Apartment (see p.16) in the Brooklyn area known as Clinton Hill occupies the top floor (ill. top left) of the brownstone row house (ill. top right). Built in 1899 as a single-family residence, it was later subdivided into floor-through apartments.

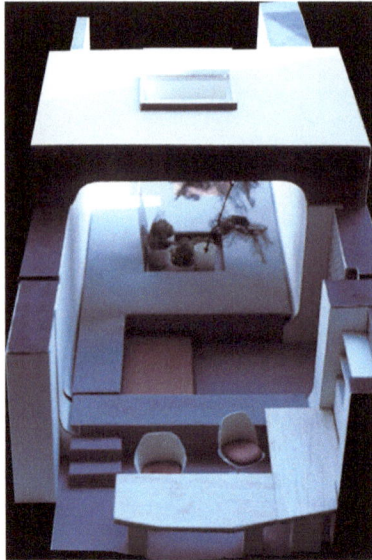

An imaginative twist for an apartment tower is Waterside Plaza (ill. middle right) decked over New York's East River. The four-tower complex connects the Kips Bay neighborhood to the river via a pedestrian plaza and esplanade. The Waterside Apartment (see p.17) is a studio (ill. middle left) on the 21st floor overlooking the East River and Queens.

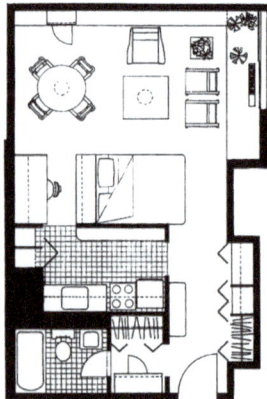

In the middle of the East River, across from midtown Manhattan and under the Queensboro Bridge is Roosevelt Island. Once called Welfare Island with jails and hospitals and now has new apartments (ill. bottom right)

that line up along a winding Main Street. The Roosevelt Island Apartment (see p.18) has one bedroom and a terrace with a view toward the river and Manhattan (ill. bottom left).

Residential Projects continued

The term "adaptive reuse" describes the concept of renovating a building originally built for a particular use and then adapting it to a new and different use. The Ottavi Firehouse Residence (see p.19) uses the 1913 firehouse shell (ill. top left) to form 3 loft-type floors (ill. top right). The building is located on Staten Island near the famed ferry to Lower Manhattan. A short walk to Hannah & Van Duzer in Tomkinsville brings you up a gentle hill and views of the harbor and Verrazano Bridge.

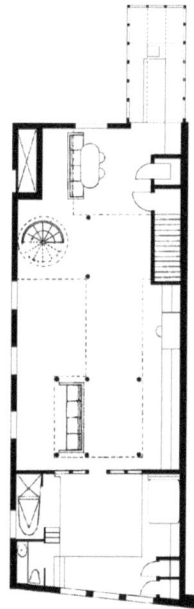

New York's Hudson River Valley is a National Heritage Area and the Westchester portion comprises most of the Historic Hudson River Towns. The Village of Croton-on-Hudson is part of the group and is just one hour to New York's Grand Central Terminal (see p.32). Above Croton Landing on Hessian Hill sits Croton Cottage Residence (see p.20) and is situated on a quarter-acre plot facing southwest with a panoramic view of the Hudson River (ill. bottom right). The tudor-style stucco cottage (ill. bottom left) and mimic garage (see p.21) was built in 1928 for a small family of modest means.

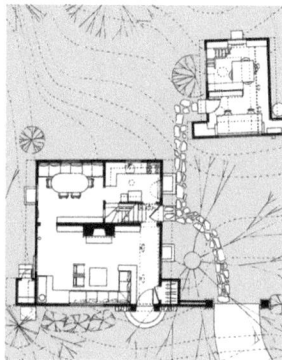

Sheltering people is a universal endeavor and the materials and methods to constuct these habitats have advanced but some qualities remain constant. An important factor that distinguishes a home from an inhospitable space is its immediate surrounding. Whether urban, suburban or rural, your home will only feel hospitable if your senses allow it to be so. A row house on a tree-lined street in the Clinton Hill Historic District is more desirable than a row house under the Brooklyn-Queens Expressway nearby. Similarly, inventive and unique highrise apartment living on the East River at Waterside Plaza and Eastwood on Roosevelt Island is more desirable than nondescript rows of project towers. Views of the New York Harbor and the Hudson River offer vistas to stir your soul.

Clinton Avenue Apartment

This renovation of a brownstone floor-through involves removing existing partitions and constructing an inner shell inside the original frame in the form of a radius-cornered tunnel. With collegue Joseph Cerami, we planned and built the tunnel to stretch the length of the row house. The space between the original walls and the white inner shell provides space for storage, built-in furniture, lighting, and controls. Room areas are divided by a series of carpeted platforms and steps.

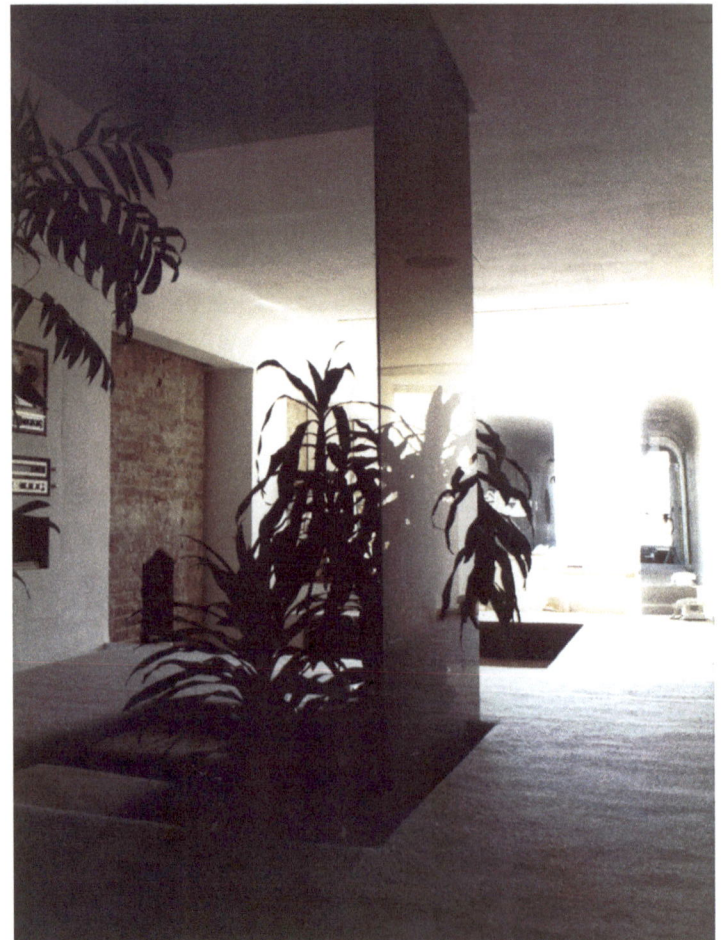

Waterside Plaza Apartment

This project poses a challenge because of the many activities that need to take place within a small studio apartment space. The plan organizes this space into activity areas: a bed/seating area, two home office areas, and a dining area. A closet is converted into a work space, and a divider is used on one side as a second storage/work space, and on the other as the headboard for the bed. A black, white, and grey color palette is used to unify the different elements.

Roosevelt Island Apartment

This apartment's interior design reflects the outlines set by Roosevelt Island master planner Philip Johnson, and the building's architect, Josef Lluis Sert. The shape of the apartment—its terrace and sight-lines—is used to direct the placement of the living and dining areas, home office, and bedroom. Inside the entrance, a flight of stairs leads into the center of the apartment. All around, dark carpeting covers the floor as well as seating and bed platforms lining the perimeter.

Ottavi Firehouse Residence

The Fire Department's deactivated firehouse "Engine #154" now has antique cars instead of fire engines displayed on the first floor and a gallery for a collection of 75 Handel lamps on the second floor as well as a collection of large "turn-of-the-century" posters in the third floor residence. The spacious living area is the centerpiece of this home. It features high ceilings and a roof terrace next to the kitchen. The master bedroom suite is partitioned by a restored frame and glass window wall and includes a carpeted platform bed and a bathroom that has a built-in tub and shower stall.

Croton Cottage Residence

This house and studio transformation is sensitive to the existing fine craftsmanship and unique elements such as heavily textured stucco both inside and out, half-round doors, and metal casement windows. In keeping with a respect for these elements, surgical alterations were employed. A series of oculus openings, open-riser stairs, and removals to expose knee-wall space open important vistas both inside and out. The cottage plan interposed in this romantic shell is based on an orthogonal grid as a

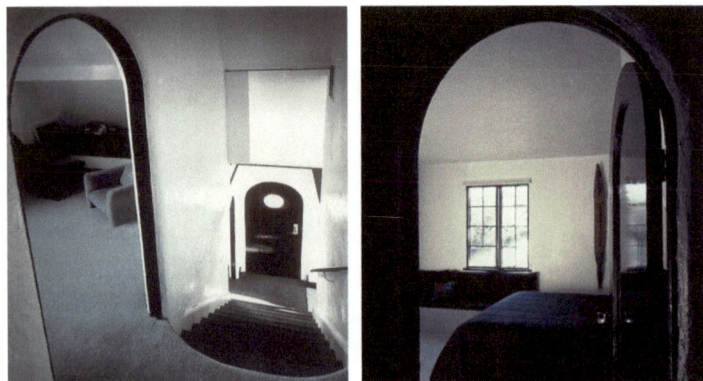

Croton Cottage continued

counterpoint to the pastoral plot of land that gradually slopes toward the river. The studio plan is a synthesis of organizing the work zones for utility and recycled material to new configurations. The vertical shelves, lateral pin-up wall, linear railing, horizontal desks, catwalk, diagonal stair are interwoven to integrate the efficiency of a small volume with geometric shapes superimposed in the space. The palette expresses contrast; white for the shell and black for the catwalk.

Corporate Projects

The workplace has evolved alongside the changing nature of work. These five projects portray a representative array of Manhattan businesses housed in a variety of buildings. From a street-level studio with an office in the back to a multi-billion dollar skyscraper next to Central Park, a place for a desk is the common denominator in today's office space. As for the desk, it can be any horizontal surface for a laptop in any location whether private or open.

Just three blocks east from Park Avenue and the innovative Lever House and Seagram Building is the E. 53rd St. Design Studio (see p.24). Next to landmarked wood frame row houses 312 & 314 (ill. top right) and carved from an alleyway at 316 (ill. top left), this narrow space is in what was originally built as a tenement in 1871. The space features a large front window to show a gallery and an office area behind the reception desk.

Grand Army Plaza is New York City's most prestigious intersection. As one of four corners of Central Park, the prominent aspect is that part of the plaza is in the park itself. Important buildings line the perimeter and across from the famed Plaza Hotel is the General Motors Building (ill. bottom right). It was designed by Edward Durell Stone and completed in 1968 with a distinctive facade of alternating vertical lines of white marble and dark windows. Inside, floor-to-ceiling bay windows are in-between solid walls. The management company giant, Arnold Palmer Enterprises/IMG (see p.25) occupies offices on the 6th floor facing the plaza (ill. bottom left). The project focuses on the core circulation area servicing the string of private offices along the windowed perimeter.

Studio space as part of the office offers the chance to combine two types of uses to form

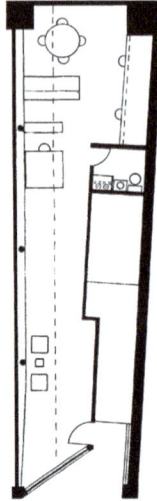

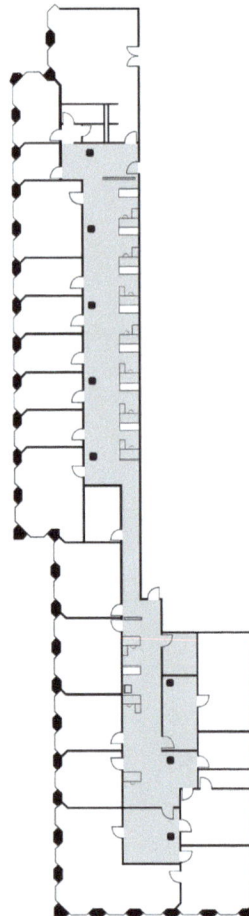

Corporate Projects continued

a new hybrid, especially if the conditions warrant an inventive creation. The Gallucci Photo Studio (see p.26) features a photo shoot space that requires special lights and equipment to be assembled and reassembled at a moment's notice for a new assignment. The Park Avenue South office building built in 1911 (ill. top left) provided ample size (both bay width and ceiling height) to accommodate the shoot space. The office and support areas are located in an adjacent bay (ill. top right).

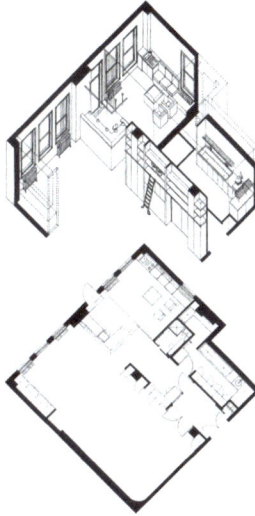

Several Manhattan neighborhoods are both mixed-use zoned and have blurred identities because they adjoin an adjacent area. 375 Hudson St. (ill. middle left) in Hudson Sq. stradles Greenwich Village and SoHo. The building was built in 1987 and occupies an entire block and provides a large floor plate (ill. middle right) for uninterrupted spaces. Saatchi & Saatchi Advertising Offices (see p.27) occupies several floors and finds the trendy area and accommodating size ideal.

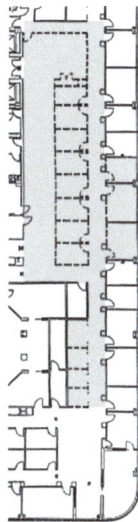

Urban visions often include rooftop terrace pavilions and gardens that overlook the city. Called penthouses, some are setbacks in the original building, others are add-ons. The 5th Avenue Penthouse Studio (see p.28) is a shed-on-a-roof with a large skylight (ill. bottom left). The original building, built in 1892, is in the Ladies Mile Historic District and near the famed Flatiron Building. The shed addition is connected to the elevator lobby via an ornate stairway (ill. bottom right).

Offices come in all shapes and sizes but the planning and design for them include some basic fundamentals, most notable that they function well. Tasks performed in these projects proceed in enlightened environs.

East 53rd Street Design Studio

This office, awarded an IBD/Interior Design Magazine design award, is a renovated street-level storefront space in midtown Manhattan. The long, narrow front portion of the space serves as a gallery for a series of fine-art exhibitions as well as design projects, while the more open back area was devoted to an office including a library and conference area. A simple vocabulary of elements helped to define and unify the interior: white walls and ceiling, dark durable carpet, Formica furniture.

Arnold Palmer Enterprises/ IMG Offices

This project requires a system of workstations for the executive support staff, as well as a redesign of the surrounding office area. The extremely long corridor for executive secretaries is also the main circulation between the reception area and private offices. Workstations in this corridor are stepped so that the Plexiglass dividers bring a spectrum of color into the windowless hallway.

Gallucci Photography Studio

Edward Gallucci, a photographer specializing in tabletop photography, leased a space that was previously occupied by a printer. The industrial space needed a renovation that would both bring light into the studio and fulfill the technical needs of his specialty. The focal point of the design is the shooting area, including the cyclorama, a backdrop with an "infinite horizon" effect for a tabletop tableau. A sequence of areas: entry, reception, office, darkroom, and workbench, are integrated in the layout.

Saatchi & Saatchi Advertising Offices

Due to ongoing changes in group composition and clientele, space planning is in constant flux, and a facility -wide effort to transition from individual offices and windowless areas to an open studio environment was initiated. This 17th floor area required the removal of selected partitions while retaining an intricate pattern of two kinds of ceilings with multiple heights.

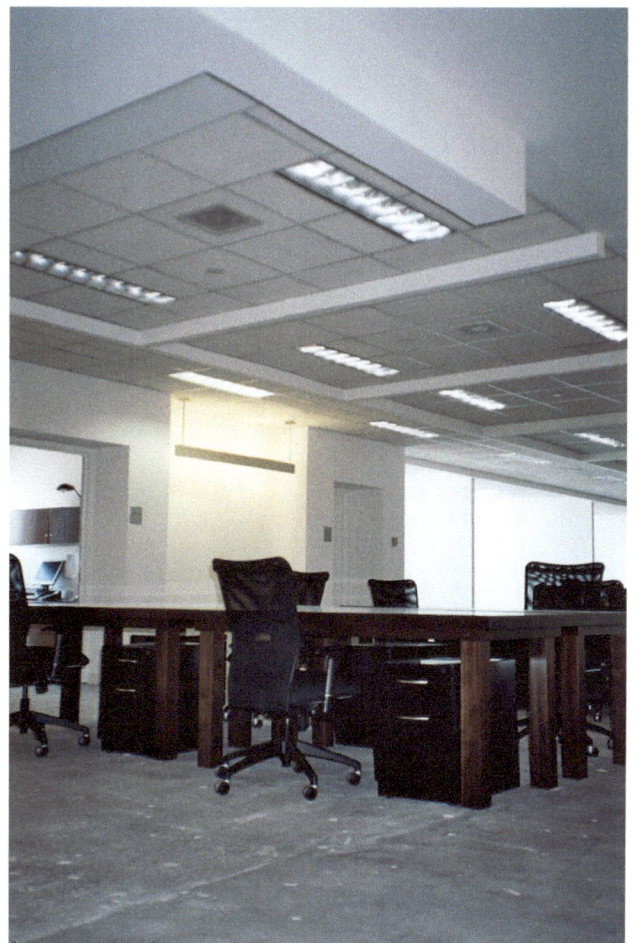

5th Avenue Penthouse Studio

What was once a photographer's studio has been transformed to an architect's office and has as its centerpiece a large, cascading skylight to fill the open-trussed main space with natural light. In many cases a photographer's studio offers features that are unique; and if treated creatively, they can be transformed for other uses. The most prominent one here is the cyclorama; it has inside radius-corner curves to form a "infinite horizon" shell and is now treated as a sculptural

Penthouse Studio continued

shape. Floating in front are Homasote panels for display. These form a series of screens that subtly subdivide the main space. The passage from the elevator to the main space takes you through a variety of environments; you climb an ornate skylit stair to an entry vestibule which faces the Empire State Building, then into an entry hallway with a kitchen off one side and a private office on the other. These spaces are small (they have a low ceiling and raised floor) and all overlook the main space.

Landmark Projects

In April, 1965, the New York City Landmarks Preservation Commission was created in response to the demolition of the famed Pennsylvania Station and other notable structures. Since then, many buildings and districts have been protected. In the spirit of preserving our past, the term "landmark" is applied here broadly and includes structures and areas not designated but are nonetheless notable. These five projects employ adaptive-reuse in order to bring new life to these landmark structures.

Grand Central Terminal (ill. top right) designed by Warren & Wetmore, Reed & Stem in 1913, was designated a NYC landmark in 1967. After a Penn Central challenge, the Supreme Court decided for it to remain protected from demolition in June, 1978. Once the Terminal was saved, ancillary spaces tucked in and around the main concourse were available for development. The "attic" of the Terminal (ill. top left) originally housed Grand Central School of Art and is adapted for Grand Central Racquetball Club (see p.32). Public access to the Terminal interior showcases the structural elements forming the Beaux Arts roof shape.

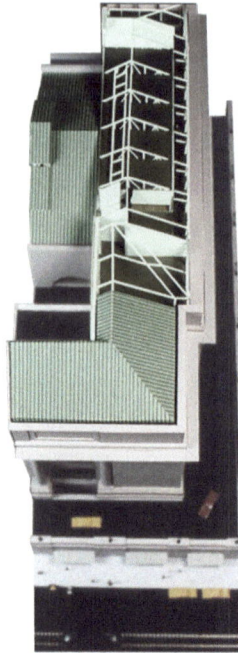

The Donnell Library Center (ill. middle right) was built on property assembled by John Rockefeller Jr. to connect Rockefeller Center to the Museum of Modern Art and designed by Aymar Embury II in 1955. Besides the circulating library and collections, there is the ITG/Information Technology Group Data Center (see p.33) that directs all things digital for the NYPL on the 5th floor (ill. middle left).

The NYC Building was built for the 1939-40 World's Fair in Queens and designed by Aymar Embury II (ill. bottom right). In the 1964-65 Fair, half was a now-defunct rink and the other is the Panorama of NYC, a model of the city and now part of the Queens Museum of Art (see p.34). Both form the new plan (ill. btm left).

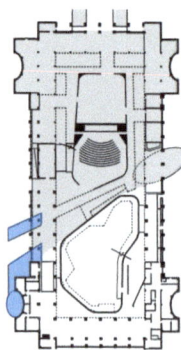

Landmark Projects continued

The morning of September 11, 2001 will always be a tragic day because of the loss of life and destruction of the World Trade Center. The site of the Twin Towers has come to be known as "Ground Zero" and in memory of that day,

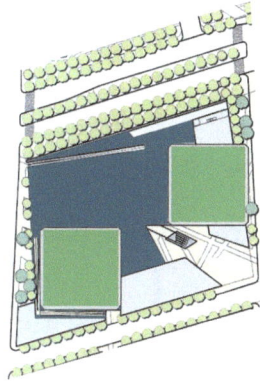

a physical memorial will be built on that ground (ill. top right). The World Trade Center Memorial project, "Memorial Walk" (see p.35) encompasses both footprints of the Twin Towers and the so-called "bathtub", the exposed foundation slurry walls and bedrock (ill. top left).

Known as the Eiffel Tower of Brooklyn, the Parachute Jump ride in Coney Island was first part of the amusement zone in the 1939-40 World's Fair in Queens (ill. bottom left). Now a designated NYC landmark as well as National Register of Historic Places, it was re-erected in the Steeplechase Amusement Park after the Fair closed. The Park closed in 1964, and the ride hasn't run since 1968 and now it stands as the primary Coney icon with an LED light show. Nestled under the Jump (ill. bottom right), the Parachute Pavilion

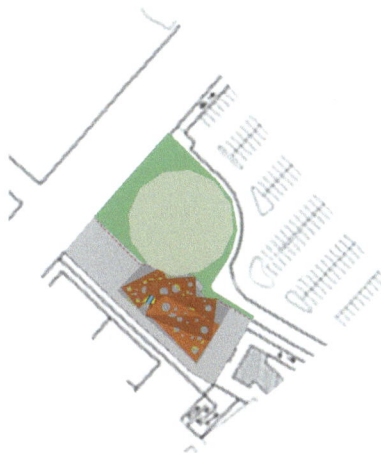

project (see p.36) mimics the deflated parachutes that used to land next to where the pavilion sits. The colorful, ornate Jump base is always in sight and is a visual connection to Coney's heyday.

As a cultural idea, the landmark preservation movement has been with us for centuries. It's no accident that Athens and Rome are filled with antiquities. Prominently, the Athenian Acropolis and the Roman Forum are the centerpieces of modern Athens and Rome respectively. A closer reading of the movement is to notice the slow accretion of modernity interwoven in all the tiny streets of very old buildings in every old quarter of every old city. The projects in this chapter as well as most of the projects in this book reflect on working with the fabric of the existing condition, the context. Here, the focus on New York City lends itself to a study in what constitutes urbanism. The indications show that urbanism leads to inventivness for new ways of life that help society make its way in the modern world.

Grand Central Racquetball Club

High above the concourse of Grand Central Terminal, the five court club under the roof trusses, includes locker rooms, sauna facilities, pro shop, lounge areas and a health food bar that all fit nicely in 10,000 square feet of space. The upper level lounge above the courts allow you to rise in the space and survey the dramatic structural elements that frame the distinctive roofline.

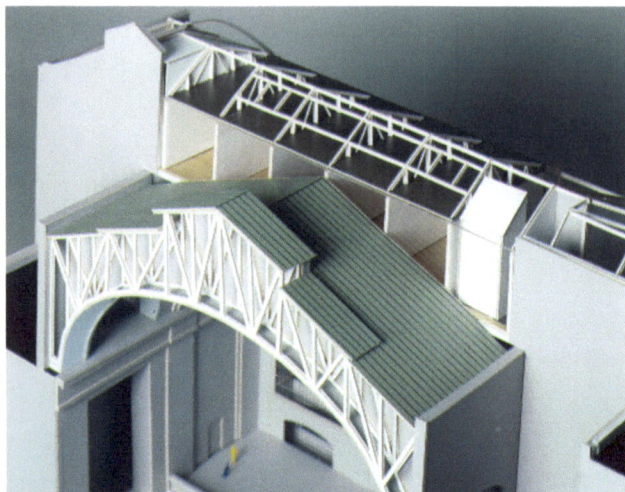

NY Public Library/ITG Data Center

The centerpiece of the data center is the computer room. All personnel require access to it and the central spine organizes an otherwise chaotic floor plan. The uniform ceiling height throughout was relieved with a second higher height that echoes the spine and creates a commons where staff and visitors can detect a sense of place. Several common work tables are in this area.

Queens Museum of Art

The centerpiece of the new half of the Museum is the multi-use gallery/theatre enclosure. A ramp surrounds the enclosure and connects to the perimeter galleries. This exo-skeleton system is inserted to contrast the new part from the existing Neo-classical architecture. A part of the roof is raised from the trusses to shine light into the atrium. The organizing element is a ramp system that connects the component spaces. These spaces are sequenced to provide a sense of dynamic procession.

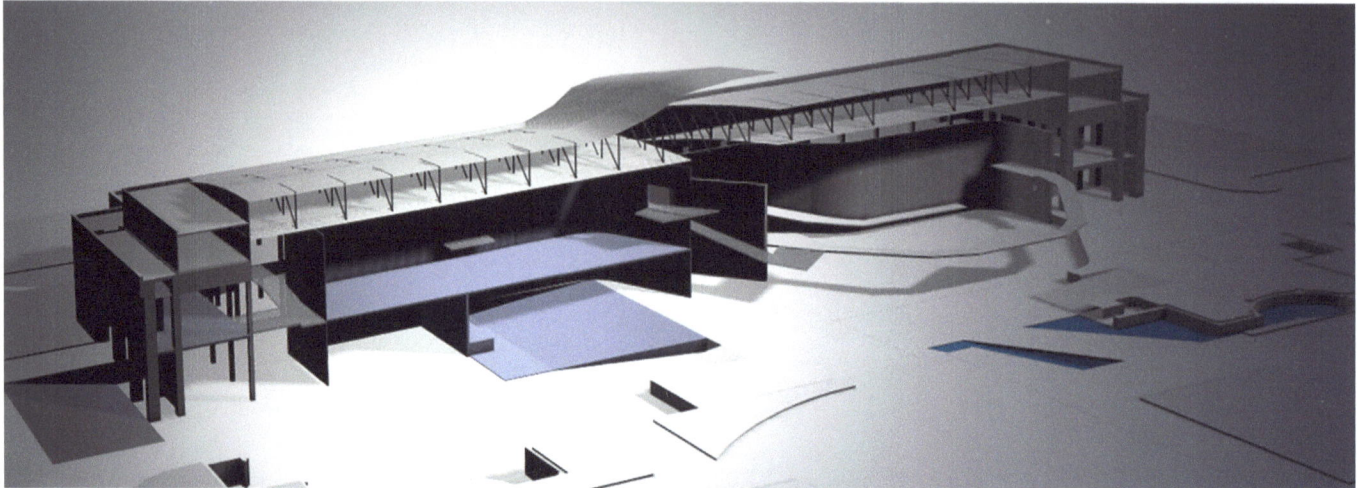

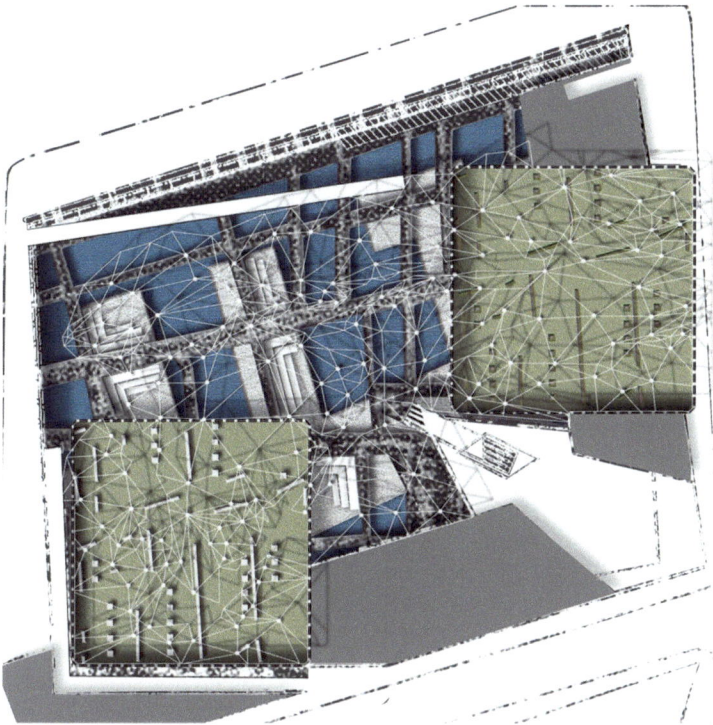

World Trade Center Memorial

The history of the Twin Tower's site is central to the Memorial. The project's design consists of "layers of history" set in an atmosphere that evokes the ruins of 9/11. The lowest layer is a reflecting pool framed by the slurry walls. Walkways and ramps are derived from the historical street pattern of the area and layered on the site for pedestrians. The footprints of the Towers are truncated structures that house the names of the deceased and its columns support a branched shroud.

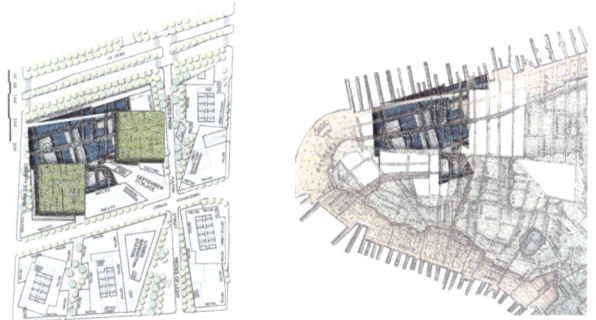

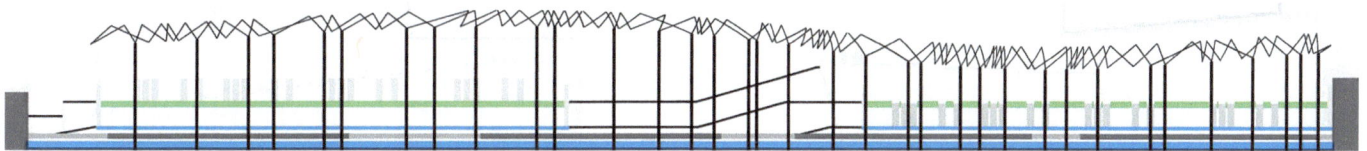

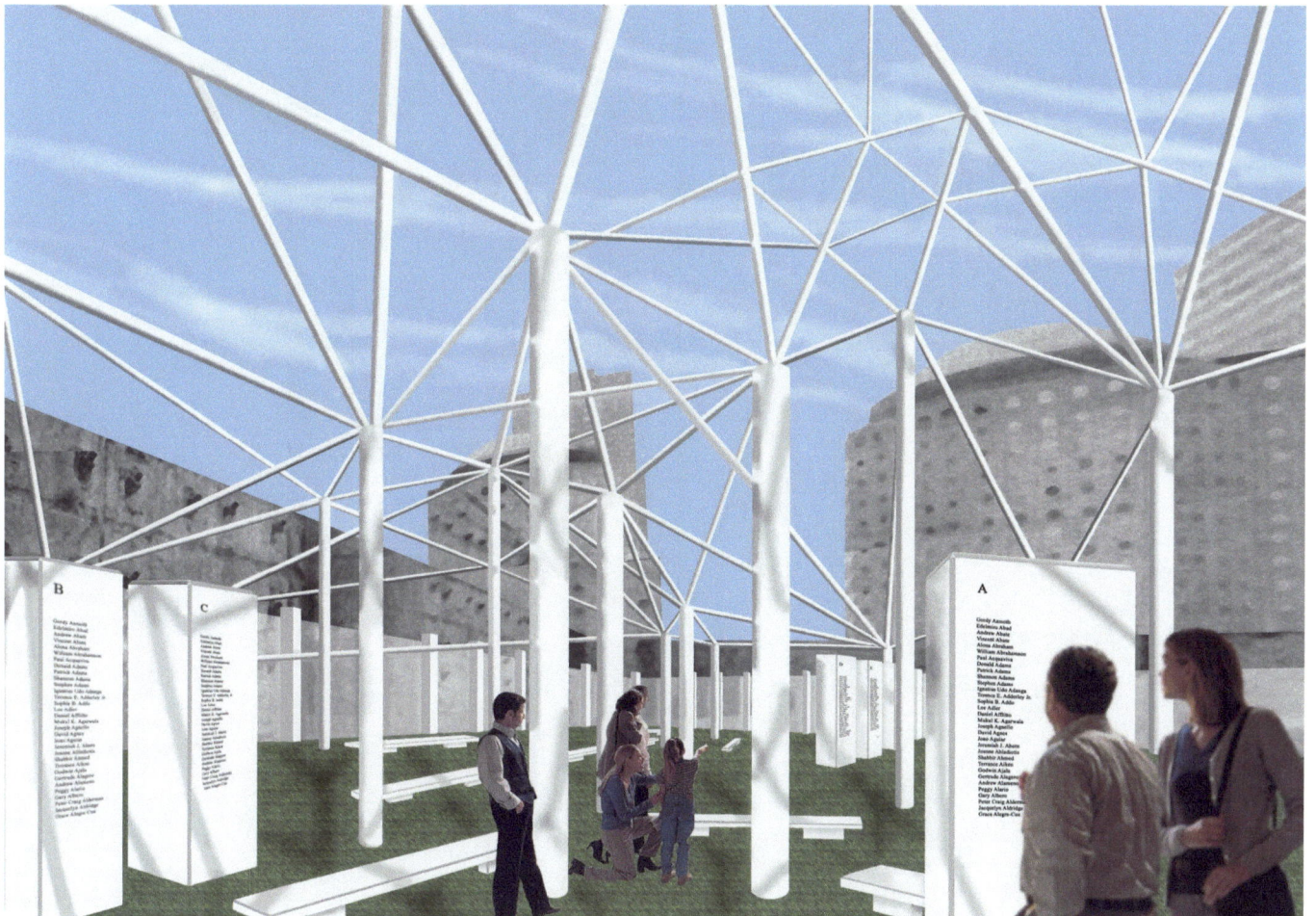

Coney Island Parachute Pavilion

The tilted trapezoidal planes of the roof elicit a kinetic atmosphere of reincarnated wind-filled parachutes, cascading in a sea-saw rhythm, setting into its landing station. Underneath the roof and inside the yellow roller-coaster-shaped perimeter wall with canopy doors, you look up through clear ellipses that punch through the roof and you catch a vision of the Parachute Jump.

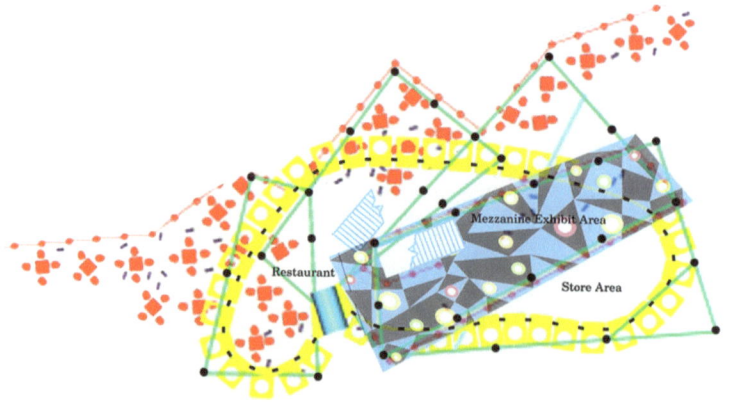

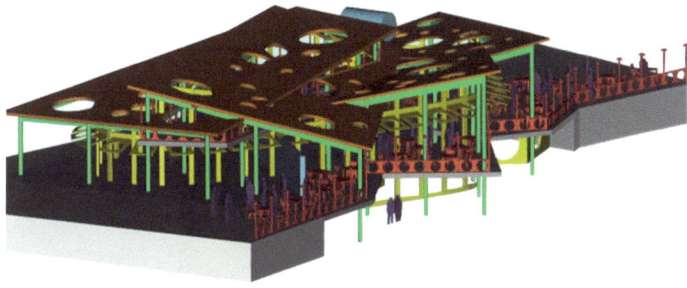

Parachute Pavilion continued

The different parts of the pavilion are situated on three levels. On the parking lot level is an entry foyer leading to the elevator, restaurant kitchen, bathrooms, and offices. The boardwalk level, the main one (open-air in season) is the restaurant and store and are divided by a mural wall in a relief surface. The third level mezzanine is a gallery. An echo of the Jump base is a clock tower. It's the elevator tower, and its motif of gears and moving parts, mimic Coney's rides and the elevator itself.

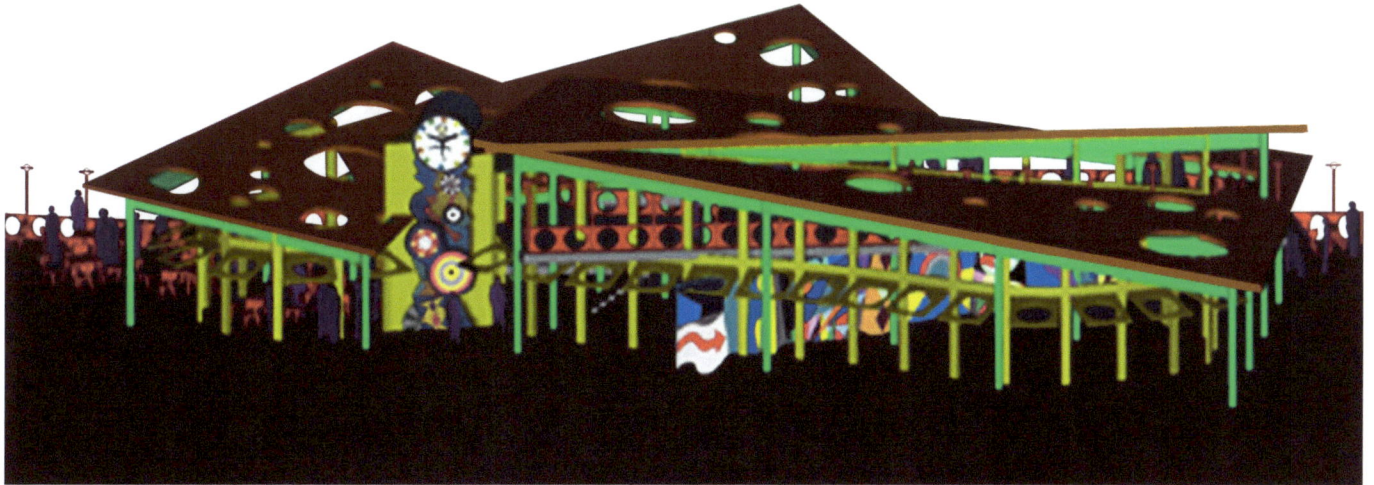

International Projects

In the tradition of the Grand Tour, the subject of this chapter is the influence of travel on the ideas and development of projects. The use of the term "travel" here is generally the notion that when venturing from home to different destinations it's an opportunity the see new things and take note. Also, not only physical travel, but a "flight of imagination" can take you to a place where you can apply a fresh perspective or point of view in order to create a new project. The world's at your feet by utilizing techniques in research for analysis. Competitions, projects for academic credit and self-initiated works can expand your horizon.

Two types of projects that serve to deepen an understanding of the world around us are plein-air drawing (outdoor urban sketching) and architectural analysis. While waiting for a train to Cambridge in Liverpool St. Station, London, England, and built in 1875, sketched a detail of the column and truss structure of the historic train shed (ill. top right).

At Pratt Institute, Michael Hollander's Architectural Analysis course prescribed three European buildings to dissect diagrammatically. Austrian architect Otto Wagner built his first villa overlooking central Vienna (ill. bottom right). The 1886 structure reflected his stature as the preeminent architect of the Vienna Secession. Classical and symmetrical, it has a modern sense, simple and white with a florish of decorative details. Museum Row along the Main River in Frankfurt, Germany is a row of historic villas across from central Frankfurt. Included are two of them retrofitted into museums and analyzed here. The Applied Arts Museum (ill. top left) by architect Richard Meier wraps the new part around an existing villa to create a courtyard. The German Architecture Museum (ill. bottom left) by architect Oswald Mathias Ungers uses the existing villa as a shell. The new parts are inserted within the existing context.

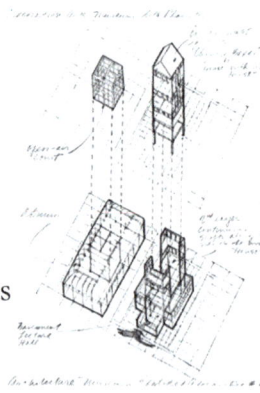

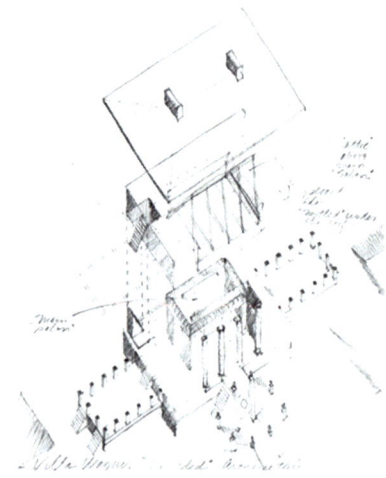

International Projects continued

These three projects highlight different aspects of how distant places inspire creative works. Architectural analysis, an academic project and an international competition offer opportunties to research and notate these sites in their contexts.

Pratt Summer Study in London, England 1970 (see p.40), led by Joe D'Urso, is an example of how a rigorous, inspired program can be a lifelong creative influence. Homebase in Evelyn Gardens, South Kensington and central to dozens of places and sites, all of them leaving a lasting impression. An important site (ill. top right) is the subject of the assigned analysis project: Spatial Transitions of Piccadilly Circus (ill. top left).

Thomas Leeser's Studio at Pratt assigned the project: Speyer Synagogue Museum (see p.41). The site in Speyer, Germany (ill. middle right) contains the ruins of a 12th century synagogue and underground bath house (ill. middle left). The project is to design a new museum by developing a formal methodology to investigate and extrapolate the history and significance of the site.

For its "Paris, France 2009" Competition, Arquitectum proposes a reinterpretation of "the new Moulin Rouge", the most famous cabaret in the world and a symbol of what is an important aspect of Parisian life. In a quest for the perfect show, a design for a new space that incorporates the latest tendencies for a new dance school (see p.42) is proffered. At the foot of Montmatre, the Moulin Rouge is in the Pigalle district (ill. bottom right). The 1889 historic red windmill (ill. bottom left) with its distinctive landmark status is central to the project and gives this chapter its unique point of view.

London/1970

One of the great cities of the world, London presents many views to sketch and study: clockwise from top left, St. Paul's Cathedral interior, Palm House at Kew Gardens, Gallery 40 at the V&A Museum and the Abbey Mills Pumping Station. The Regent Street Crescent is the most dramatic architectural feature in and around the Piccadilly Circus area. The series of photographs below are in sequence for a stroll and show the various spatial transitions that occur as you look around.

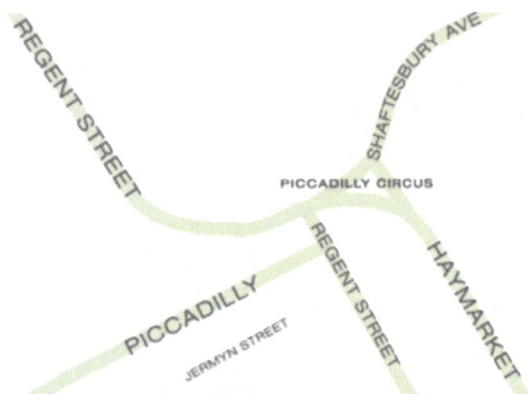

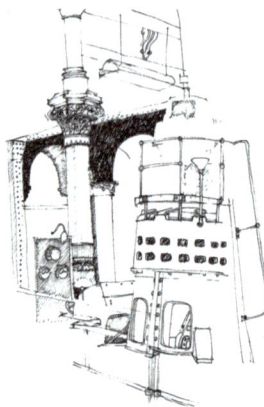

Speyer Synagogue Musuem

The archaeological layering of each cultural epoch: the Roman encampment, the Christian Romanesque Speyer Cathedral and the realignment of the main axis to it, the ancient Jewish community surrounding the site and Nazi Germany/Kristallnacht, are metaphorically reconstructed. Then, by the use of analogy, scaling and superimposition, synthesize the morphology and context of the site with the text and expression of the museum. The experience of entering the museum and navigating the various paths is to evoke a distressing sense of disconnect from the larger community. Like the past ghetto in the shadow of the more prominent Christian community and Speyer Cathedral, the museum seeks to simulate transgression by a forced disconnect from the current typical context.

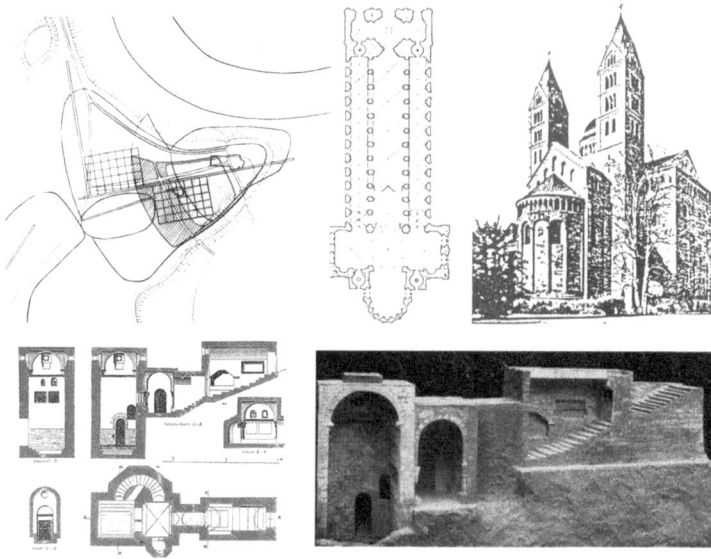

Moulin Rouge Dance School

The prominent windmill symbol provides the main idea.
By extruding it downward in the form of a periscope,
the circular mirror is angled to offer pedestrians a view
of the auditorium stage below grade. The angled facade
gradually reveals more of the windmill as it rises. Inside,

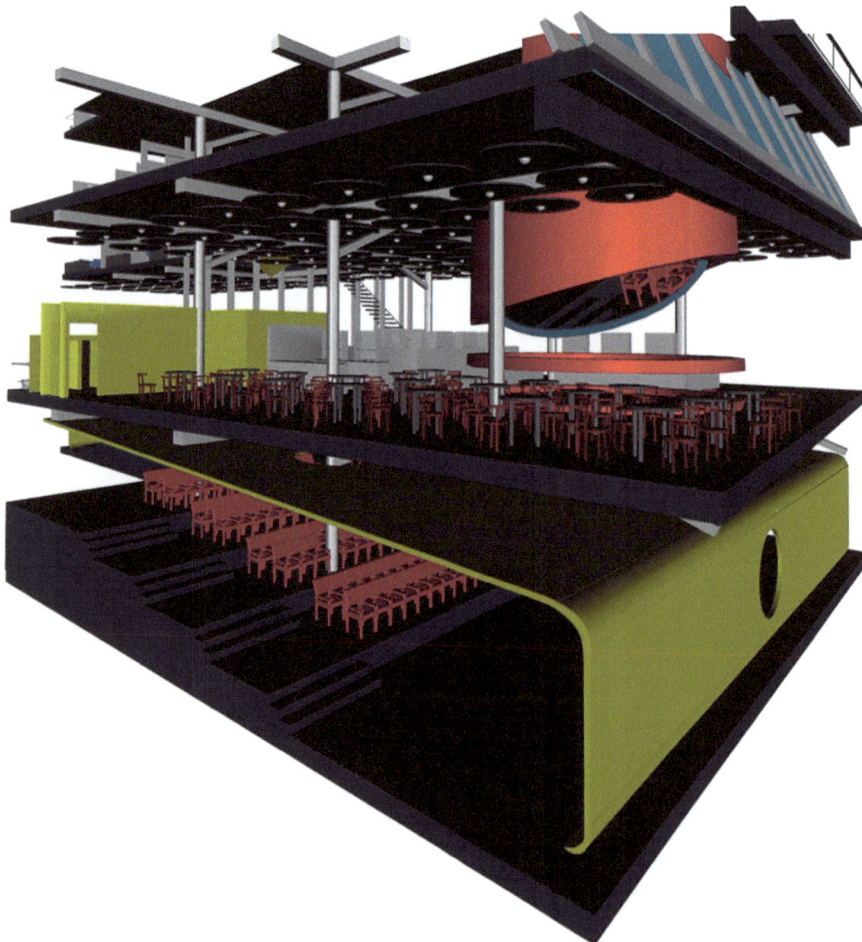

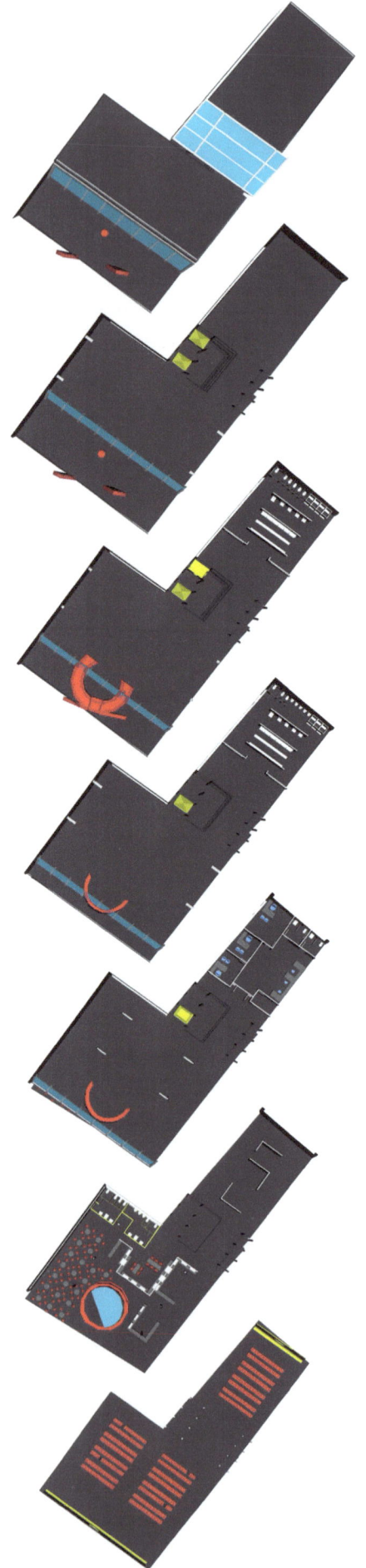

Moulin Rouge continued

it is carved into and surrounded by terraces to allow people to navigate it. The new building provides loft-type spaces and has a central atrium topped with a skylight. Throughout, glass for transparency is used (curtain wall, railings, etc.). The overall impression imparted is that a large structure is woven inbetween adjacent buildings with the deconstructed windmill icon floating in relief and highlighted for all to see.

Credits

It's fortunate that some of the most talented and accomplished artists have incorporated their art in these projects and photographers have photographed these projects. Their art helps to convey the salient features of each space. With a concern for the sequence of views, they compose the spatial story.

Cover: Croton Cottage, Photo: Paul Warchol

Title Page: CIUSA Freak Bar, Photo: Paul Warchol

Table of Contents: (top to bottom) CIUSA Freak Bar, Photo: Paul Warchol; Croton Cottage, Photo: Paul Warchol; Gallucci Photo Studio, Photo: Ed Gallucci; Grand Central Racquetball Club model, Photo: Ed Gallucci

Page 6: (middle right) Fruity's Restaurant, Photo: Richard Champion

Page 7: (top left) The Left Bank Restaurant, Photo: Robert Perron; Artwork (sign/logo): Zahor/Mitnick; (bottom left) CIUSA Freak Bar, Photo: Paul Warchol

Page 9: Fruity's Restaurant, Photos: Richard Champion; Artwork (paintings & Plexiglas construction): John Walker

Page 11: (middle to bottom) The Left Bank Restaurant, Photos: Robert Perron; Artwork (wall hangings): Kathleen Ferguson-Tusa

Pages 12-13: CIUSA Freak Bar, Photos: Paul Warchol

Page 15: (bottom left) Croton Cottage, Photo: Paul Warchol

Page 17: Waterside Plaza Apartment, Photos: Tom Haar; Artwork (painting): Giuseppe San Filipo; (framed photos): Bill Kontzias

Page 18: Roosevelt Island Apartment, Photos: Elliot Fine

Page 19: (top) Ottavi Firehouse Residence, Article: New York Spaces, 9/06, Siren Call, p.90

Page 20: Croton Cottage Residence, Photos: Paul Warchol

Page 21: Croton Cottage Residence, Photos: Peter Paige; (bottom left) Photo: Paul Warchol

Page 23: (bottom left) 5th Avenue Penthouse Studio, Photo: Scott Frances

Page 24: East 53rd Street Design Studio, (top right, bottom left) Photos: Bill Kontzias; (bottom right) Photo: Jaime Ardiles-Arce; Artwork (stained glass): Kathleen Ferguson-Tusa; (paintings): Giuseppe San Filipo

Page 26: Gallucci Photo Studio, Photos: Ed Gallucci

Page 28-29: 5th Avenue Penthouse Studio, Photos: Scott Frances

Page 30: (top left) Grand Central Racquetball Club model, Photo: Ed Gallucci

Page 32: (middle left & right) Grand Central Racquetball Club model, Photo: Ed Gallucci

Page 37: Coney Island Parachute Pavilion, Artwork (clocktower & mural): Philomena Marano

Page 49: (lower right) Coney Island Kiosk/Clocktower, Artwork (clocktower): Philomena Marano

Back Cover: Roosevelt Island Apartment, Photo: Elliot Fine

Chronology

This illustrated timeline was first designed in 2003 as a 30th Anniversary brochure mailer titled "Beginning in...."(this page)..."Then....30 Years of Achievement & Recognition"(see pp.46-47). The timeline is continued to 2016 (see pp.48-49).

Special art classes at Dyker Hts. J.H.S. with art instructor Rochelle Giumenta. Thanks to her encouragement, I attended Saturday art classes at Pratt Institute and applied to the High School of Art & Design.

THE CREATIVE WORLD

Philip Tusa

Beginning in .....

| 1963 | 1964 | 1965 | 1966 | 1967 | 1968 | 1969 | 1970 | 1971 | 1972 | 1973 |

Architecture at the H.S. of Art & Design with Irwin Muller of Ammann & Whitney, and Harold Krisel of Skidmore, Owings, & Merrill. Together, they introduced me to the field of architecture. In addition to the curriculum, they arranged for me to visit Philip Johnson for a Random House project and encouraged me to apply to Pratt Institute.

New York, New York

Philip Johnson—Builder of America's new cities.

Interior Design at Pratt with professor Joe D'Urso, a protege of Ward Bennett.

Pratt Summer 1970 Study Program in London with D'Urso. Visit James Stirling, Bath, Soane Museum and other significant people & places. Project: Piccadilly Circus/Regent Crescent study.

www.philiptusa.com

Then....
30 Years of
Achievement
&

New York
Photo District News

A Monthly Newspaper For The Professional Photographer

Diary of a Farewell

Gallucci

VOICE

FOOD

People
ARE TALKING ABOUT

INTERIOR DESIGN

IBD / INTERIOR DESIGN
COMPETITION WINNER

Office/Gallery
for an Interior Designer

How Much is an MBA Degree Really Worth?
Gael Greene on Regine, the Queen of Nightclubs
New York

The Underground Gourmet
By Milton Glaser and Jerome Snyder
FRUITT'S

Architecture at *Pratt* with
Raimund Abraham, Thomas
Leeser, Diane Lewis, Ed
Mitchell, Richard Scherr,
Hanford Yang, et al.

Established *Philip Tusa Design Inc.*

| 1973 | | 1975 | | 1977 | | 1979 | | 1981 | | 1983 | | 1985 | | 1987 | |
| 1974 | | 1976 | | 1978 | | 1980 | | 1982 | | 1984 | | 1986 | | 1988 |

Bachelor of Fine Arts in Environmental/Interior Design
Pratt Institute

Recognition

The Left Bank

HIGH-TECH
THE INDUSTRIAL STYLE AND
SOURCE BOOK FOR THE HOME

STRUCTURAL
ELEMENTS

RAILINGS

Interiors

RESTAURANT
DESIGN

APARTMENT LIFE

THE
APARTMENT
BOOK

THE ENGINEERED APARTMENT

THE LEFT BANK

Times
Tower
Design
Competition

Juried at *Municipal
Art Society*

Chronology continued

INTERIOR DESIGN

News

Exhibited in *Village Summerfest* on behalf of Croton Teen Council

Croton-on-Hudson Skateboard Park

Exhibited in Entrant's Show at **QMA**

Queens Museum of Art Design Competition

INTERIOR DESIGN

York Construction News

Racquetball Courts For Grand Central Terminal

Style

JOX & SOX

GRAND CENTRAL RACQUETBALL CLUB

GREENPORT WATERFRONT

PARK COMPETITION

Exhibited in Entrant's Show at **Legion Hall**

Skyline Studio

1987	1989	1991	1993	1995	1997	1999	2001	2003
1988	1990	1992	1994	1996	1998	2000	2002	

Master of Architecture
Pratt Institute

AT WORK AT HOME
Design Ideas for Your Home Workplace

Established *Philip Tusa, Architect*

Bachelor of Architecture
Pratt Institute

INTERIOR DESIGN

On Roosevelt Island

New York News

World Trade Center's History Central to One Architect's Design

Memorial Walk

Exhibited at *Fordham University* on behalf of Van Alen Institute

The New York Public Library

EAST RIVER DESIGN COMPETITION

TERRA-COTTA ARTIFACT MUSEUM

Presented and Approved by NYPL / *ITG Data Center* Directors

WORLD TRADE CENTER SITE MEMORIAL COMPETITION

Madison Square Design Studio Renovation

The Municipal Art Society of New York
MAS NYC Voice for the future of our city.

IMAGINE CONEY

ABOUT   OVERVIEW   SUBMIT IDEA   GALLERY   RESOURCES & LINKS

Introduction

Philip Tusa, Architect
www.philiptusa.com

Introduction:
Steeplechase Park
1. Times Tower Competition
2. Greenport Park Competition
3. Croton Neo-Arcadia Riverfront
4. Croton Skateboard Park
5. Parachute Pavilion Competition
6. Coney Island USA Freak Bar &
    Museum Gift Shop

Key Plan   Imagine Coney

ARCHITECTURE FOR ARCH

NEW YORK SPACES

Siren CALL

METROPOLIS **P/O/V**

Public Forums to Save Coney Island

2003

The [Ultimate] Urban Makeover

THE PARACHUTE PAVILION:
an open design competition for Coney Island

PARACHUTE PAVILION

CONEY ISLAND THE PARACHUTE PAVILION COMPETITION

ZOË AYRES AND JONATHAN CHACE-LITANT, EDITORS

ARCHITECTURE COMPETITION
THE NEW DANCE SCHOOL FOR THE MOULIN ROUGE

PARÍS. FRANCE **2009**

Roof
Elevated Shaft
Artisate Skylight
Museum

5th Floor:
Training Room 3
Exterior Terrace
for social events

Training Room 2
Perspective

4th Floor:
Women's Dressing
Rooms
Training Room 2

3rd Floor:
Men's Dressing
Room
Training Room 1

2nd Floor:
Administration
Commissary
Longitudinal Section

1st Floor:
Museum
Recreation
Box offices
Seasonal Stores
Cafeteria
Entrance Hall

Below Grade:
Auditorium 2
Exterior Terrace/Atrium
for social events
Auditorium 1

MOULIN ROUGE
Dance School &
Museum   108943

Knoll
What is YOUR space
WINNERS!!

Inc. + **Architizer**
WORLD'S COOLEST OFFICES

Chronology continued

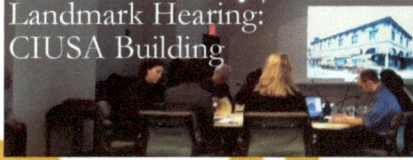

Croton Cottage Dining Room Renovation

Pratt

200 Willoughby Avenue
Brooklyn, NY 11205
School of Architecture
Office of the Dean
Telephone:
718 399-4304
Facsimile:
718 399-4315

December 14, 2009

Philip Tusa

Dear Philip,

As one of our most distinguished alumni of the School of Architecture, I am writing to you with a special request. This year our two accredited architecture programs are being reviewed by the National Architecture Accrediting Board. Preparations for this review include extensive reporting and the assembly of several exhibits.

2016

Of critical importance is an exhibition and documentation of the work and achievements of our most important alumni, and I am writing to you and approximately forty other graduates to ask for your help and participation in this show. In order to participate, I simply ask that you send a photograph of yourself, a 500 to 700 word statement or short curriculum vitae with your career ach[...] and two to four images of your work. These images may include covers of books or repo[...] in conferences or events, images of projects, photographs of buildings, or any other ima[...]ts an important aspect of your work. We will take the images and asse[...] on Higgins Hall. Attached is a d[...] in

[...] and [...] I [...] ou

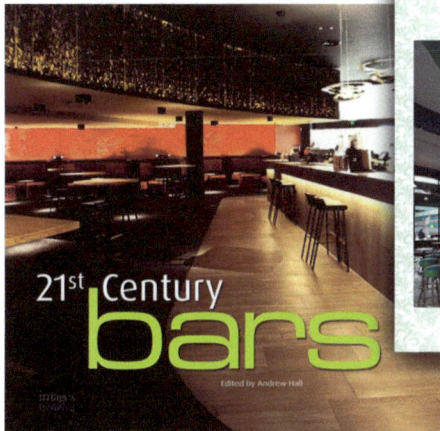

Thomas Hanrahan, Dean
School of Architecture.

21st Century bars

FREAK BAR
BROOKLYN, NEW YORK, USA
Philip Tusa, Architect

Coney Island Kiosk/Clocktower

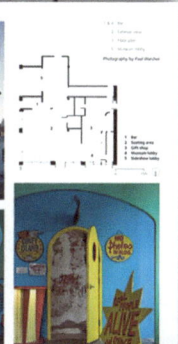

NYIT Exhibit